POCKET PICTORIAL GUIDE TO

The
Lake District

Val Corbett

MYRIAD

LONDON

Keswick Backed by Skiddaw and overlooking Derwent Water, Keswick is perfect for exploring the northern Lakes. The Keswick Launch Company runs cruises around Derwent Water starting at the Keswick boat landing.

Ashness Bridge Barrow Beck flows under this ancient packhorse bridge on the road to Watendlath. This treasured view, with Derwent Water and Skiddaw in the far distance is photographed by thousands of visitors every year.

Borrowdale Stretching from the head of Derwent Water to Seathwaite, Borrowdale is walled in by steep crags on all sides. A short distance upstream at "the Jaws of Borrowdale" the valley squeezes between Grange Fell and Castle Crag, leaving just enough room for the river to snake through. Grange-in-Borrowdale (left) is near the southern end of the lake. The Borrowdale Show takes place in mid September.

Castlerigg Situated south of Keswick, the Castlerigg Stone Circle is one of Britain's most important neolithic monuments.

7

Buttermere This remote valley can be reached either from the Newlands or Honister passes. It is close to low-lying water meadows where cattle grazed, giving Buttermere its name. The village consists of little more than a farm and two hotels, The Bridge and The Fish. Crummock Water lies just across the fields.

Bassenthwaite Lake Situated at the foot of Skiddaw, the word "lake" is included in Bassenthwaite's name – all the other lakes in the region are "meres", "tarns" or "waters". Its peaceful, reedy east shore has abundant bird-life and, in summer, is blessed with great drifts of wildflowers.

Crummock Water Looking across the Loweswater Valley to Crummock Water (above) with the lake sandwiched between the mountains of Grasmoor and Melbreak. In the far distance is the distinctive profile of Great Gable.

Melbreak & Crummock Water The side valley of Rannerdale (right) leads away from Crummock Water and is famous for the bluebells which carpet its slopes in spring. At the end of the lake are the forbidding slopes of Melbreak with the peak of Grasmoor beyond.

Windermere Many visitors catch their first view of the Lake District as they drive over the crest above Windermere. The lively village is the perfect base for exploring the area and the lake bustles with the comings and goings of small boats and pleasurecraft including the *Osprey* (above). Built in 1902 this is one of the lake's historic cruisers. There are wonderful views of the lake and surrounding fells from Queen Adelaide's Hill, on the eastern shore.

Bowness On the shores of Windermere this bustling lakeside village retains a great deal of its original charm. Many of the grand Victorian houses built by 19th-century industrialists as holiday homes now survive as hotels.

Troutbeck The Queen's Head is at the centre of the village which stretches for more than a mile along a side road off the Kirkstone Pass.

Ambleside This is a bustling small town with a lively student community. The oldest part of the town, the route up to the Kirkstone Pass, has some attractive old houses and streets to explore. Peggy Hill, off North Road and sharply uphill from Stock Bridge, is a good place to start a walk through the town. Beyond it are the old mill buildings (right) complete with waterwheel. Higher up are the waterfalls in Stock Ghyll Park where you can see the remains of other watermills in the area.

Ambleside Bridge House on the Rydal Road straddles Stock Beck and is owned by the National Trust.
Waterhead Established in 1845 at the northernmost point of Windermere, launches and steamers sail all year to Bowness and Lakeside from this busy ferry terminal.

Rydal The village of Rydal is famous for its association with William Wordsworth, the great Romantic poet. Rydal Hall, an imposing mansion, is now used as a conference centre. Rydal Mount (right) was the poet's home for the last four decades of his life. In contrast to the simplicity of Dove Cottage (his previous home in Grasmere) Rydal Mount is grand and spacious. The house contains family possessions, portraits and furniture. The gardens, with the poet's summerhouse, are laid out as they were when Wordsworth lived there.

Elterwater Located four miles west of Ambleside, Elterwater (left) is scenically placed at the entrance to the Langdale valley. The visitor's first view, coming either from Grasmere or Ambleside, is always impressive with the Coniston Fells and Langdale Pikes forming a dramatic background.

Chapel Stile The fortified tower of Holy Trinity church rises above the village with Silver Howe as a backdrop.

The Langdale valleys Home to the rocky-topped Langdale Pikes, the beautiful valleys of Great and Little Langdale (below) are remote and wild, and a particular favourite with climbers.

Grasmere Famous as the home of William Wordsworth for the most creative period of his life, Grasmere is at the heart of the Lake District. The poet lived at Dove Cottage (right) and its tiny rooms are still much as they would have been when he lived there with his sister Dorothy and wife Mary. All three are buried in the Church of St Oswald in the village and their gravestone is a place of pilgrimage for lovers of the Lakeland poets. The view below looks across the lake from one of the beaches on its southern shore.

Ullswater Located between Pooley Bridge in the north and Glenridding in the south, Ullswater is regarded by many as the most beautiful of the English lakes. The view above is from Glencoyne looking east towards the slopes of Place Fell. The much photographed Pooley Bridge boathouse lies close to the bustling village of the same name. The view shows the quiet edge of the lake looking across to Arthur's Pike and Bonscale Pike. Boats belonging to the Ullswater Steamer Company link Pooley Bridge with Howtown and Glenridding and connect with spectacular walks on the eastern side of the lake.

Wordsworth's daffodils After walking along the Glencoyne side of Ullswater, Dorothy Wordsworth wrote in her diary entry of 15th April 1802, "I never saw daffodils so beautiful..." Her brother included some of her description in his famous poem *I wandered lonely as a cloud*, also known as *Daffodils*.
Patterdale On the road between the Kirkstone Pass and Ullswater, Patterdale (right) is a magnet for walkers. The view (below) looks across Glencoyne Farm from the former miners' cottages at Seldom Seen. This view was a favourite of Queen Victoria and remains little changed since her day.

Glenridding The largest village on Ullswater, Glenridding lies near the southern end of the lake on the road to the Kirkstone Pass. At weekends, if the weather is good, crowds of walkers leave Glenridding as they set off for Striding Edge. For the less ambitious, the historic Ullswater steamers *Raven* and *Lady* (below) will ferry passengers to Howtown or Pooley Bridge. The southern lakeshore walk from Howtown to Glenridding is reckoned to be one of the best in the Lake District with constantly changing vistas.

Pooley Bridge The landing stage at Pooley Bridge, on the north shore of Ullswater.

Lowther Castle The spectacular Lowther Castle lies five miles south of Penrith. This Gothic ruin fell into disrepair as a result of the high-spending lifesyle of the "Yellow" Earl, the 5th Lord Lonsdale.

Askham Described by the famous fell-walker Alfred Wainwright as "the most attractive village in Westmorland" the pretty cottages in Askham line a wide and picturesque village green. The road through the village climbs steadily for nearly a mile to Askham Fell.

Hartsop This unspoilt village (right) is located in a sheltered side-valley near Brothers Water. In the past the area was busy with mining, quarrying and milling. It is worth taking the short walk along the track to the Haweswater Reservoir.

Haweswater This remote reservoir was constructed in the 1930s by building the massive dam wall at Burbanks and enlarging the existing lake. The reservoir supplies Manchester with drinking water. Submerged beneath the water lies the old village of Mardale, drowned when the valley was flooded.

High Street The mountain (left) is named High Street. The Romans built a road here which follows the ridge across its flat summit. The road originally connected Roman forts near Penrith and Ambleside.

33

Hawkshead Situated midway between Windermere and the northern end of Coniston Water, Hawkshead is a compact maze of buildings, dominated by the church of St Michael's and All Angels. A short, sharp climb from Hawkshead leads to the summit of Latterbarrow (right) from which there are dramatic panoramic views to the west across the town to the Coniston Fells. In the near distance is Blelham Tarn with the northern reaches of Windermere in the distance.

Lakeside One mile north of Newby Bridge, Lakeside (below right) is a popular spot and is always busy with steam trains and pleasurecraft.

Esthwaite Water At the heart of Beatrix Potter country, Esthwaite Water is close to the villages of Near and Far Sawrey. Hill Top (below left) is situated in Near Sawrey. It was the home of Beatrix Potter who bought the house with the earnings from her first children's books. It is now owned by the National Trust.

Coniston The Old Man of Coniston dominates the landscape above the town. The slopes of the slate grey mountain are scarred by the legacy of old mineworkings – copper was extracted here for more than 500 years. Famous people associated with the town include John Ruskin, Arthur Ransome and Donald Campbell who made his attempt on the world water-speed record here.

Coniston The photograph (left) shows High Bank Grounds, the farm which was the setting for the writer Arthur Ransome's famous children's book *Swallows and Amazons*. The photograph below is taken from Brantwood, the home of the critic and social reformer John Ruskin; it was considered by him to be the finest in the Lake District. This photograph was taken on a still September morning; the peaks of the Old Man of Coniston and Weatherlam tower above the village of Coniston. The restored steam yacht *Gondola* (right) plies Coniston Water from the pier to Brantwood.

Wasdale This remote valley in the far west is a hidden corner of the Lake District. Lying between Gosforth, Santon Bridge and Wast Water, Nether Wasdale (left) is the tiniest of settlements. The dramatic photograph (below) of Wasdale from Great Gable is taken from a vantage point close to the Westmorland Cairn, built in 1876 by two Westmorland brothers to mark what they regarded as the finest mountain viewpoint in the Lake District. Lying a few hundred yards south, and out of sight of the summit of Great Gable, it clings to the mountain's rim above a startling drop.

Wasdale Head More of a hamlet than a true village, this is the only clutch of buildings for many miles around. Wasdale Head has a magnificent setting just north-east of Wast Water in an area of dramatic mountains which include Scafell. The tiny Church of St Olaf, close to the track at Wasdale Head, is almost entirely surrounded by ancient yews. In the graveyard are memorials to climbers. A nearby path leads to the start of the ascent of Great Gable. The pack-horse bridge (right) lies behind the Wasdale Head Inn at the far end of the lake.

Eskdale This narrow valley links the heart of the Lake District with the west coast of Cumbria. At the end of the valley lie Scafell, Scafell Pike, Esk Pike and Bowfell – some of the giant peaks of the Lake District. The view (above) shows Brotherilkeld Farm and the Upper Eskdale valley from the slopes of Harter Fell.

Hardknott Fort In a dramatic location below Hardknott Pass is the Roman fort of Hardknott. The fort guarded the strategic road which ran from the harbour at Ravenglass over the mountains to Ambleside.

Wasdale This dramatic view is the first glimpse of Wast Water that most visitors experience as they approach from the west.